HELEN EXLEY GIFTBOOKS
thoughtful giving starts here...

OTHER GIFTBOOKS BY HELEN EXLEY

Wisdom for the New Millennium
... and wisdom comes quietly
Words on Calm
Words on a Simple Life
Wishing You Happiness
Words on Solitude and Silence

Published simultaneously in 2001 by Exley Publications Ltd
in Great Britain, and Exley Publications LLC in the USA.

2 4 6 8 10 12 11 9 7 5 3 1

Copyright © Helen Exley 2001
The moral right of the author has been asserted.

ISBN 1-86187-298-4

Created and selected by Helen Exley.
Illustrated by Juliette Clarke.
Printed in China.

Exley Publications Ltd,
16 Chalk Hill, Watford, Herts WD19 4BG, UK.
Exley Publications LLC,
232 Madison Avenue, Suite 1409, NY 10016, USA.
www.helenexleygiftbooks.com

A SPECIAL GIFT OF

PEACE
&
CALM

Illustrated by Juliette Clarke

A HELEN EXLEY GIFTBOOK

EXLEY
NEW YORK • WATFORD, UK

I WISH YOU PEACE

Deep peace, pure white of the moon to you;

Deep peace, pure green of the grass to you;

Deep peace, pure brown of the earth to you;

Deep peace, pure grey of the dew to you,

Deep peace, pure blue of the sky to you!

Deep peace of the running wave to you,

Deep peace of the flowing air to you,

Deep peace of the quiet earth to you.

FIONA MACLEOD

–

I wish you joy and peace and deep
contentment.
And always, always, love.

PAMELA DUGDALE

–

I wish you quiet sleep, dreams of meadows
deep in flowers and grass,
of oceans calm and flecked with silver
of islands hushed by gentle waves
of countries of your own invention
of easy talk with friends
of roads leading to a reunion
of sorrow comforted
of hope restored.

PAM BROWN, B.1928

—

LET PEACE ENFOLD YOU

Shed the day's anxieties, one by one.
No need to hurry. Let the body drowse.
Unwind, little by little.
Still the mind.
Breathe slow
– until at last the busy world retreats
and leaves you in a gentleness,
a stillness,
a refuge of peace and calm.

PAM BROWN, B.1928

–

Listen in deep silence.
Be very still and open your mind....
Sink deep into the peace that waits for you
beyond the frantic, riotous thoughts
and sights and sounds of this insane world.

FROM "A COURSE IN MIRACLES"

–

Quieten your mind.
Quieten your heart.
Let peace enfold you.

PAM BROWN, B.1928

A HEALING SILENCE...

And silence, like a poultice, comes
To heal the blows of sound.

OLIVER WENDELL HOLMES (1809-1894)

—

There are times when we stop.
We sit still. We lose ourselves
in a pile of leaves or its memory.
We listen and breezes from a whole
other world begin to whisper.

JAMES CARROLL, B.1943

–

The clear river curves around our village:
these long summer days are beautiful, indeed.

Swallows swoop from the eaves,
the gulls all flock to the water.

... This medicine is all a sick man needs.
What man could ask for more?

TU FU

–

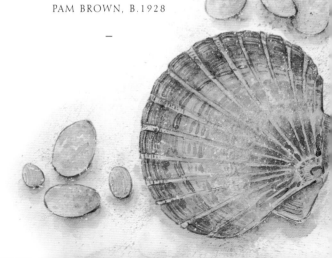

TAKE THE GENTLE PATH

If there is tumult in your heart
seek out tranquillity
– a calm and moonlit sea,
a place of peace,
a gentleness of landscape
and let their quietness flow
through you,
and wash your care away.

PAM BROWN, B.1928

–

The miracle comes quietly into the mind
that stops an instant and is still.

FROM "A COURSE IN MIRACLES"

—

Nothing is so strong as gentleness;
nothing so gentle as real strength.

ST. FRANCIS DE SALES (1567-1622)

—

Ultimately we have just one moral duty: to
reclaim large areas of peace in ourselves, more
and more peace, and to reflect it toward others.
And the more peace there is in us, the more
peace there will be in our troubled world.

ETTY HILLESUM (1914-1943)

—

May peace and peace and peace be everywhere.

THE UPANISHADS (c.900-600 B.C.)

—

"SACRED IDLENESS..."

Don't hurry don't worry,
you're only here for a short visit.
So be sure to stop and smell the flowers.

WALTER HAGAN

–

What life can compare to this?
Sitting quietly by the window,
I watch the leaves fall and the flowers bloom,
as the seasons come and go.

HSUEH-TOU (982-1052)

–

Work is not always required.
There is such a thing as sacred idleness,
the cultivation of which is fearfully neglected.

GEORGE MACDONALD (1824-1905)

–

ONE QUIET DAY

LET US SPEND ONE DAY
AS DELIBERATELY AS NATURE,
AND NOT BE THROWN OFF THE TRACK
BY EVERY NUTSHELL AND MOSQUITO'S WING
THAT FALLS ON THE RAILS.
LET US RISE EARLY AND FAST,
OR BREAK FAST, GENTLY AND WITHOUT
PERTURBATION.... IF THE BELL RINGS,
WHY SHOULD WE RUN?

HENRY DAVID THOREAU (1817-1862)

—

Let us not therefore go
hurrying about and collecting
honey, bee-like, buzzing here
and there impatiently from
a knowledge of what is to be
arrived at. But let us open
out leaves like a flower... budding
patiently... and taking hints from
every noble insect
that favours us with a visit.

JOHN KEATS (1795-1821)

—

HOME – A PLACE OF CALM

Sweet Stay-at-Home, sweet Well-Content.

WILLIAM HENRY DAVIES (1871-1940)

–

Even in the heart of a city
there can be a place of calm.
Doors shut and curtains closed, a light
against the dark, wrapped round in dear,
accustomed things we can withdraw
and find ourselves again.

PAM BROWN, B.1928

–

I laugh when I hear that the fish in the water
is thirsty. You don't grasp the fact that what
is most alive of all is inside your own house;
and so you walk from one holy city
to the next with a confused look!

KABIR (1440-1518), FROM "THE KABIR BOOK"

"I AM GONE INTO THE FIELDS..."

I leave this notice on my door
For each accustomed visitor:
"I am gone into the fields
To take what this sweet hour yields;
Reflection, you may come tomorrow.
... Expectation, too, be off!
Today is for itself enough."

PERCY BYSSHE SHELLEY (1792-1822)

—

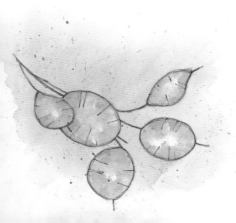

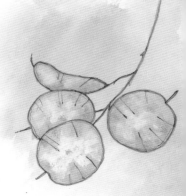

And so, while others
miserably pledge
themselves to the
insatiable pursuit of
ambition and brief
power, I will be stretched
out in the shade, singing.

FRAY LUIS DE LEÓN
(c.1527-1591)

Days tumbled on days, I was in my overalls,
didn't comb my hair, didn't shave much...
I was living the happy life of childhood again....
I was as nutty as a fruitcake and happier.
Sunday afternoon, then, I'd go to my woods
with the dogs and sit and put out my hands
palms up and accept handfuls of sun boiling
over the palms.

JACK KEROUAC (1922-1969),
FROM "THE DHARMA BUMS"

SERENITY, THE GREATEST TRUTH

Serenity is neither frivolity, nor complacency,
it is the highest knowledge and love,
it is the affirmation of all reality being awake
at the edge of all deeps and abysses.
Serenity is the secret of beauty and the real
substance of all art.

HERMANN HESSE (1877-1962)

–

The greatest revelation is stillness.

LAO-TZU (6TH CENTURY B.C.)

–

To a mind that is still the whole
universe surrenders.

CHUANG TZU

–

Contentment is the philosopher's stone, which
turns all it touches into gold; the poor are rich
with it, the rich are poor without it.

PROVERB

WORKING TOWARDS PEACE

To watch the corn grow, and the blossoms set;

to draw hard breath over ploughshare or spade;

to read, to think, to love, to hope, to pray –

these are the things that make people happy.

JOHN RUSKIN (1819-1900)

–

For the past eighty years I have started each day in
the same manner. It is not a mechanical routine
but something essential to my daily life.
I go to the piano, and I play two preludes and fugues
of Bach. I cannot think of doing otherwise. It is a
sort of benediction on the house. But that is not
its only meaning for me. It is a rediscovery of the
world of which I have the joy of being a part.
It fills me with awareness of the wonder of life,
with a feeling of the incredible marvel of being
a human being.

PABLO CASALS (1876-1973),
FROM "JOYS AND SORROWS"

—

TRUST
SURRENDER

You do not need to
leave your room....
Remain sitting at your table
and listen. Do not even listen,
simply wait. Do not even wait,
be quite still and solitary.
The world will freely offer itself
to you to be unmasked. It has
no choice. It will roll in
ecstasy at your feet.

FRANZ KAFKA (1883-1924)

Serenity is active. It is a gentle and firm participation with trust.
Serenity is the relaxation of our cells into who we are and a quiet celebration of that relaxation.

ANNE WILSON SCHAEF

–

Contentment... comes as the infallible result of great acceptances, great humilities – of not trying to make ourselves this or that... but of surrendering ourselves to the fullness of life – of letting life flow through us.

DAVID GRAYSON (1870-1946)

Calm
is a clear well
that you may
draw from
whenever you
have need.

MAYA V. PATEL, B.1943

WITHIN OURSELVES
THERE IS A SILENCE
INTO WHICH THE WORLD
CANNOT INTRUDE.
THERE IS AN ANCIENT PEACE
YOU CARRY IN YOUR HEART
AND HAVE NOT LOST.

FROM "A COURSE IN MIRACLES"

–

Deep in the soul, below pain, below all
the distraction of life, is a silence vast and
grand – an infinite ocean of calm, which
nothing can disturb; Nature's own exceeding
peace, which "passes understanding". That
which we seek with passionate longing, here
and there, upward and outward; we find at
last within ourselves.

C.M.C. QUOTED BY R.M. BUCKE

Nothing is worth more than this day.

JOHANN WOLFGANG VON GOETHE (1749-1832)

–

We tend to be alive in the future, not now.
We say, "Wait until I finish school and get my
Ph.D degree, and then I will be really alive."
When we have it, and it's not easy to get,
we say to ourselves, "I have to wait until
I have a job in order to be really alive."
And then after the job, a car. After the car,
a house. We are not capable of being alive
in the present moment. We tend to postpone
being alive to the future, the distant future,
we don't know when. Now is not the moment
to be alive. We may never be alive at all in
our entire life.

THICH NHAT HANH, B.1926

–

IT IS GOOD TO BE ALONE IN A GARDEN
AT DAWN OR DARK SO THAT ALL ITS SHY
PRESENCES MAY HAUNT YOU AND POSSESS
YOU IN A REVERIE OF SUSPENDED THOUGHT.

JAMES DOUGLAS

Over all the mountaintops is peace.
In all treetops you perceive scarcely a breath.
The little birds in the forest are silent.
Wait then; soon you, too, will have peace.

JOHANN WOLFGANG VON GOETHE (1749-1832)

*Leave home
in the sunshine:
Dance through a meadow –
Or sit by a stream
and just be.
The lilt of the water
Will gather your worries
And carry them down
to the sea.*

J. DONALD WALTERS

–

THE PEACE OF BEING AT ONE WITH NATURE

The morning sun, the new sweet earth
and the great silence.

T.C. MCLUHAN

–

I lay in a meadow until the unwrinkled serenity
entered into my bones, and made me into one
with the browsing kine, the still greenery,
the drifting clouds, and the swooping birds.

ALICE JAMES (1848-1892)

–

Once you have heard the meadowlark
and caught the scent of fresh-plowed earth,
peace cannot escape you.

SEQUICHIE

–

DRAW AWAY

I can't bear a journey to the village –
I'm too contented here.
I call my son to close the wooden gate.

Thick wine drunk in quiet woods,
green moss,
jade gray water under April winds –
and beyond: the simmering dusk
of the wild.

TU FU

... THERE IS A LUXURY IN BEING
QUIET IN THE HEART OF CHAOS.

VIRGINIA WOOLF (1882-1941)

–

In green old gardens, hidden away
From sight of revel and sound of strife....
Here may I live what life I please
Married and buried out of sight.

VIOLET FARRE

–

IT WILL BE ALL ONE

Life is eating us up.
We shall be fables presently.
Keep cool:
it will be all one
a hundred years hence.

RALPH WALDO EMERSON (1803-1882)

—

Too many people, too many demands,
too much to do; competent, busy, hurrying
people – it just isn't living at all.

ANNE MORROW LINDBERGH (1906-2001)

–

Do not let trifles disturb your tranquillity
of mind. Life is too precious to be sacrificed
for the nonessential and transient.

GRENVILLE KLEISER

–

Why should we live with such hurry and waste
of life?... Men say that a stitch in time saves
nine, and so they take a thousand stitches
today to save nine tomorrow.
As for *work*, we haven't any of any consequence.
We have the Saint Vitus' dance, and cannot
possibly keep our heads still.

HENRY DAVID THOREAU (1817-1862)

THE LAKE ISLE OF INNISFREE

I will arise and go now, and go to Innisfree,
And a small cabin build there,
of clay and wattles made:
Nine bean-rows will I have there,
a hive for the honey-bee,
And live alone in the bee-loud glade.

And I shall have some peace there,
for peace comes dropping slow,
Dropping from the veils of the morning
to where the cricket sings;
There midnight's all a glimmer,
and noon a purple glow,
And evening full of the linnet's wings.

I will arise and go now,
for always night and day
I hear lake water lapping with
low sounds by the shore;
While I stand on the roadway,
or on the pavements grey,
I hear it in the deep heart's core.

WILLIAM BUTLER YEATS (1865-1939)

—

I wish you quiet sleep,
good dreams,
happy awakenings.

PAM BROWN, B.1928

—

QUIET NIGHT

Lie gently in the dark
and listen to the rain pattering against the glass,
the swish of passing cars,
the hush of leaves.
Renounce decisions, speculation,
the tug of time.
The world beyond the window
enfolds your silence,
holds you softly. Sleep.

PAM BROWN, B.1928

—

Come away from the din. Come away to the
quiet fields, over which the great sky stretches,
and where, between us and the stars, there lies
but silence; and there, in the stillness let us
listen to the voice that is speaking within us.

JEROME K. JEROME (1859-1927)

What is a *Helen Exley Giftbook*?

Helen Exley has been creating giftbooks for twenty-six years, and her readers have bought forty-one million copies of her works, in over thirty languages. Because her books are all bought as gifts, she spares no expense in making sure that each book is as thoughtful and meaningful a gift as it is possible to create: good to give, good to receive. The themes of personal peace and wisdom are very important in Helen's life, and she has now created several titles on these themes.

Team members help to find thoughtful quotations from literally hundreds of sources, and the books are then personally created. With infinite care, Helen ensures that each illustration matches each quotation, that each spread is individually designed to enhance the feeling of the words, and that the whole book has real depth and meaning.

You have the result in your hands. If you have loved it – tell others! We'd rather put the money into more good books than waste it on advertising when there is no power on earth like the word-of-mouth recommendation of friends.

Helen Exley Giftbooks
16 Chalk Hill, Watford, Herts WD19 4BG, UK
232 Madison Avenue, Suite 1409, New York, NY 10016, USA
www.helenexleygiftbooks.com

Acknowledgements: The publishers are grateful for permission to reproduce copyright material. Whilst every reasonable effort has been made to trace copyright holders, the publishers would be pleased to hear from any not here acknowledged. PABLO CASALS: from *Joys and Sorrows* by Albert Kahn. © Albert Kahn 1970. THICH NHAT HANH: from *Being Peace* (1987) by Thich Nhat Hanh with permission of Parallax Press, Berkeley, California. ETTY HILLESUM: from *An Interrupted Life – The Diaries of Etty Hillesum 1941-1943*. JACK KEROUAC: from *The Dharma Bums* reprinted by permission of Sterling Lord Literistic Inc. © 1986 by Jack Kerouac. ANNE MORROW LINDBERGH: from *Bring Me A Unicorn*, published by Harcourt Brace Jovanovich, 1971, 1972. J. DONALD WALTERS: from *"There's Joy in the Heavens"*, published by Crystal Clarity Publishers. W.B. YEATS: "The Lake Isle of Innisfree" from *The Poems of W.B. Yeats: A New Edition* edited by Richard J. Finneran. Reprinted by permission of A.P. Wyatt on behalf of Michael B. Yeats. PAM BROWN, PAMELA DUGDALE, MAYA V. PATEL: used by permission © 2001.